ONE GOD, THREE FAITHS

Owen O'Sullivan OFM Cap

One God,
Three Faiths

columba

First published in 2002 by
the columba press
55A Spruce Avenue, Stillorgan Industrial Park, Blackrock, Co Dublin

Designed by Bill Bolger
Origination by The Columba Press
Printed in Ireland by ColourBooks Ltd, Dublin

ISBN 1 85607 349 1

Acknowledgements
The publishers and the author gratefully acknowledge the permission of the Trustees of the Chester Beatty Library, Dublin, for permission to use the illustrations in this book which are in their copyright.

Contents

To my sister, Clare,
with respect and affection;
credit where credit is due.

Preface

The three great monotheistic religions of humanity are Judaism, Christianity and Islam, and they appeared in history in that chronological order. This book does not seek to make a comparison of the three faiths, and it would be wrong to understand it as such. It does not, for example, present an adequate summary of either Judaism or Christianity. The book is an introduction: it is meant to whet the appetite, not to satisfy it. For a fuller understanding, the reader is invited to go to the sources – not just the written or oral sources but also the tradition as it is lived at present in the three communities of faith represented here.

Most readers are likely to be from Europe or North America and will probably already have some familiarity with the sacred writings of Judaism and Christianity, namely, the Old and New Testaments respectively. The starting point for the selection of texts here is the Qur'ân (Koran). My reason for choosing this approach is that in Europe and North America the Judeo-Christian tradition has a long history, but Islam is less well-known. Muslims are a growing minority there and it seems desirable that a start be made on understanding some of the basic elements of Islam and how it relates to Judaism and Christianity. What is offered is a series of extracts from the sacred text(s) of those religions, allowing them to speak for themselves. This book seeks to contribute to a dialogue and to mutual understanding between members of all three religions.

The task of selection was not without difficulty. My concern was to choose representative samples of the major themes of Islam and, where possible, to find broadly corresponding texts in the Jewish and Christian scriptures. This inevitably leads to some distortions which believers of those latter faiths may find unsatisfactory. For instance, there is nothing about the central Jewish theme of Covenant, or of the equally central Christian themes of Incarnation and Redemption.

I was anxious not to select in a polemical fashion, by juxtaposing, for example, some of the gentle texts of the Old Testament with some of the harsh texts of the Qur'ân, or vice versa. Neither would it have been representative to have chosen only 'nice' texts from all three religions, as if some hard sayings that jar on modern sensibilities were not part of all their scriptures.

With all three religions, no selection can be adequate in illustrating the full range of its tradition. This book is meant to be no more than a starting point, and it is

offered to readers in a spirit of dialogue
in the hope of encouraging a step
towards respecting and accepting each
other despite our real differences.

> Let us have –
> unity in essentials,
> freedom in what is not essential,
> and, in all things, charity.

*A Mamluk Qur'ân
from Cairo. Early four-
teenth century. Chester
Beatty Library, Dublin.*

Introduction to Islamic Texts

For Muslims the Qur'ân is not simply a sacred book, nor even the most sacred book. It would be nearer the truth to say that, in the minds of Muslims, the Qur'ân occupies the place that Jesus (rather than the Bible) occupies in the minds of Christians. Indeed, Muslims are 'People of the Scripture' more than either Jews or Christians are. Muslims accept both the Torah (the Old Testament) and the Gospel as coming from God (see the Qur'ân 5:44, 47), though without the same authority as the Qur'ân.

A clarification is necessary: 'The Qur'ân was revealed to Muhammad in Arabic only. So, any Qur'ânic translation, either in English or in any other language, is neither a Qur'ân, nor a version of the Qur'ân, but rather it is only a translation of the meaning of the Qur'ân. The Qur'ân exists only in the Arabic in which it was revealed.' (Ibrahim, page 54)

Unless otherwise noted, the Islamic texts cited are from the translation done by Mohammad Marmaduke Pickthall (see Acknowledgements). The numbers refer to *surah* (chapter) and verse: thus Qur'ân 5:44, 47 means *surah* 5, verses 44 and 47 of the Qur'ân. In a few cases I adapted the translation slightly in order to bring it into line with contemporary English usage. It sometimes displayed a quaint, archaic character evocative of the style of the King James Bible. For example, I changed 'Vie with one another in good works' (Qur'ân, 5:48) to 'Compete with one another in good works' and 'aught' to 'anything' in the Qur'ân 4:171. My concern was to attune the translation to modern usage.

Along with citations from the Qur'ân are some from the *hadith*. These are reliably transmitted reports by the prophet Mohammad's companions of what he said, did, or approved of, and are understood as explaining the divine message.

In addition, learned members of the community can use their discretion in finding answers to questions that have not been dealt with in the Qur'ân and the *hadith*. They also are entitled to expand the meaning of the Qur'ânic passages to take account of newly arising situations. However, their conclusions should in no way clash with the clear teachings of the Qur'ân and the *hadith*.

Introduction to Jewish Texts

The Bible accepted by Jews is the same as what Christians call the Old Testament, with the exception of the books of Sirach (also known as Ecclesiasticus) and Tobit. For traditional Jews the first five books of the Old Testament, that is, Genesis, Exodus, Leviticus, Numbers and Deuteronomy – collectively known as the Torah (Hebrew: teaching, law) – are *the* definitive self-revelation of God. To them they are like what Jesus is to Christians. But no Jews, whether conservative or liberal, regard the New Testament or the Qur'ân as divinely inspired.

Jews read the Bible in the context of the rabbinic tradition which, at least for orthodox Jews, is assumed to have its roots in the revelation by God to Moses on Mount Sinai. This reference to tradition can mean that the plain sense of a verse is not always definitive. A verse has to be read in its context and by reference to other texts which deal with a similar topic, and to the tradition of the community. An example is the oft-quoted (and misquoted!) sentence, 'Anyone who maims another shall suffer the same injury in return: fracture for fracture, eye for eye, tooth for tooth; the injury inflicted is the injury to be suffered.' (Leviticus 24:20) At first sight this may seem like a command to exact vengeance. But

Jewish tradition has never understood this as a warrant for the exaction of vengeance. It has seen the text as *limiting* retribution for injuries received, the limits to be determined by a court.

The rabbinic tradition is developing constantly down to the present time, in the context of the lived experience of the Jewish community of faith as it endeavours to be true to the Covenant. This tradition is dynamic but, at the same time, maintains essential continuity with its past. One expression of this evolving character of tradition is in the prayer books of the Jewish people. These are among the best expressions of what Jewish faith means to the ordinary man or woman. The Psalms are the prayer book of the Old Testament but they have been supplemented down the centuries by many other anthologies, such as C. G. Montefiore and M. Loewe, *A Rabbinic Anthology*, (Macmillan, London, 1938).

In this short anthology, I have included extracts from Sirach since, although it is regarded by Jews as not being definitive of the Jewish tradition, it does illustrate it well.

Introduction to Christian Texts

Christians accept the Old Testament as being divinely inspired, and it forms the first and largest part of their Bible. It is followed by the New Testament which tells about the life and teaching of Jesus Christ, his death and resurrection. Christians do not accept the Qur'ân as part of God's revelation to humanity.

Christians see Jesus as the Word of God in human form. Similarly, they see the Bible as being divine words in human language. They take into account the conditions of the time and culture of the sacred writers, their literary conventions and the modes of feeling, speaking and narrating which were then current.

Generally, Christians use three criteria in interpreting the Bible:
To be attentive to the content and unity of the whole of scripture. This would mean, for example, neither isolating a text from its context, nor ignoring other texts on a similar theme;
To read the scripture within the living tradition of the whole Christian community, its life and teaching;
To take account of the coherence of the truths of the Christian faith among themselves and within the overall plan of God's revelation.

Traditionally, Christians read a text in four ways or senses:

The literal sense: here, the word 'literal' has a technical meaning. It does not mean 'the obvious sense', but rather that which the author wished to convey;

The allegorical sense: for instance, the act of Moses in leading the people of Israel into the promised land from slavery by crossing the Red Sea may be seen as an allegory of Christ leading people from slavery to sin to the freedom of the children of God through the water of baptism;

The moral sense: scripture was written for our instruction and is meant to lead the reader to a better moral life;

The anagogical sense looks at where a text leads. (Greek: *anagogé*, leading). So, the kingdom of God on earth is seen as a sign that points to its fulfilment in heaven.

Summary of the Faith

Islam

'There is no God to worship except Allah (God), Muhammad is Messenger (Prophet) of Allah (God).' Ibrahim, page 31.

The Five Pillars of Islam are:
    the testimony of faith, 2:177;
    prayer, 24:56;
    giving *zakat* (support for the needy), 24:56;
    fasting during the month of Ramadan, 2:185;
    the pilgrimage to Makkah [Mecca] once in a lifetime for those who are able, 3:97.

'Worship none save Allah, and be good to parents and to relatives and orphans and the needy, and speak kindly to humankind, and establish worship and pay the poor-due.' 2:83

Judaism

'Hear, O Israel: The Lord our God is one God. You shall love the Lord your God with all your heart, and with all your soul, and with all your might. Keep these commandments that I am commanding you today in your heart. Recite them to your children and talk about them when you are at home and when you are away, when you lie down and when you rise. Bind them as a sign on your hand, fix them as an emblem on your forehead, and write them on the doorposts of your house and on your gates.' Deuteronomy 6:4-8

The Ten Commandments:
'I am the Lord your God; you shall have no other gods before me.
You shall not make wrongful use of the name of the Lord your God.
Observe the sabbath day and keep it holy.
Honour your father and your mother.
You shall not murder.
Neither shall you commit adultery.
Neither shall you steal.
Neither shall you bear false witness against your neighbour.
Neither shall you covet your neighbour's wife.
Neither shall you covet your neighbour's goods.' *From* Deuteronomy 5:6-21

'What does the Lord require of you but to do justice, and to love kindness, and to walk humbly with your God?' Micah 6:8

Christianity

'If you confess with your lips that Jesus is Lord, and believe in your heart that God raised him from the dead, you will be saved.' Romans 10:9

Jesus taught them, saying:
  'Blessed are the poor in spirit, for
  theirs is the kingdom of heaven.
  Blessed are those who mourn, for
  they will be comforted.
  Blessèd are the meek, for they will
  inherit the earth.
  Blessed are those who hunger and
  thirst for righteousness, for they will
  be filled.
  Blessed are the merciful, for they will
  receive mercy.

  Blessed are the pure in heart, for
  they will see God.
  Blessed are the peacemakers, for
  they will be called children of God.
  Blessed are those who are persecuted
  for righteousness' sake, for theirs is
  the kingdom of heaven.'
  From Matthew 5:1-10

'In everything do to others as would have
them do to you; for this is the law and
the prophets.' Matthew 7:12

Fragments of a papyrus of the Gospel of St Luke. c 250 AD. Chester Beatty Library, Dublin.

Teaching on God

Islam

'There is no true God but God, and Muhammad is the Messenger (prophet) of God.' Ibrahim, page 52

'Your God is One God; there is no God save Him, the Beneficent, the Merciful.' 2:163

'Unto Allah belong the sovereignty of the heavens and the earth and whatsoever is in them, and He is able to do all things.' 5:120

'Serve Allah, you have no other God save Him.' 11:61

'Not a leaf falls but He knows it.' 6:59

'All power belongs to Allah. Unto Him good works ascend and the pious deed he exalts.' 35:10

Judaism

'Hear, O Israel: The Lord our God is one God. You shall love the Lord your God with all your heart, and with all your soul, and with all your might. Keep these commandments that I am commanding you today in your heart. Recite them to your children and talk about them when you are at home and when you are away, when you lie down and when you rise. Bind them as a sign on your hand, fix them as an emblem on your forehead, and write them on the doorposts of your house and on your gates.' Deuteronomy 6:4-8

'I am the Lord your God who brought you out of the land of Egypt, out of the house of slavery; you shall have no other gods before me.' Exodus 20:2-3

'There is no one like the Lord our God.' Exodus 8:10

'God ... has been my shepherd all my life.' Genesis 48:15

'The Lord is my strength and my might, and he has become my salvation; this is my God, and I will praise him, my father's God, and I will exalt him. The Lord is a warrior; the Lord is his name.' Exodus 15:2-3

'The Lord, the Lord, a God merciful and gracious, slow to anger, and abounding in steadfast love and faithfulness, keeping steadfast love for the thousandth generation, forgiving iniquity and transgression of sin ...' Exodus 34:6-7

Christianity

'The grace of the Lord Jesus Christ, the love of God, and the communion of the Holy Spirit be with all of you.'
2 Corinthians 13:13

'In the beginning was the Word, and the Word was with God, and the Word was God. All things came into being through him, and without him not one thing came into being. What has come into being in him was life, and the life was the light of all people. The light shines in the darkness, and the darkness did not overcome it.
The true light, which enlightens everyone, was coming into the world. He was in the world, and the world came into being through him; yet the world did not know him. He came to what was his own, and his own people did not accept him. But to all who received him, who believed in his name, he gave power to become the children of God, who were born, not of blood, or of the will of the flesh, of the will of man, but of God. And the Word became flesh and lived among us, and we have seen his glory, the glory as of a father's only son, full of grace and truth. From his fullness we have all received, grace upon grace. The law indeed was given through Moses; grace and truth came through Jesus Christ. No one has ever seen God. It is God the only Son, who is close to the Father's heart, who has made him known.' John 1:1-5, 9-14, 16-18

'Our Father.' Matthew 6:9

CREATION BY GOD

Islam

'Allah creates what He wills. If he decrees a thing, He says to it only: Be! And it is.' 3:47

'He (Allah) is the All-Wise Creator.' 36:81

'Our Lord is He who gave to everything its nature, then guided it aright.' 20:50

'We created man and We know what his soul whispers to him, and We are nearer to him than his jugular vein.' 50:16

'I created ... humankind only that they might worship me.' 51:56

Judaism

'In the beginning ... God created the heavens and the earth .... God saw everything that he had made, and indeed it was very good.' Genesis 1:1, 31a

Christianity

'From him [God] and through him and to him are all things. To him be the glory forever. Amen.' Romans 11:36

'One day he [Jesus] got into a boat with his disciples, and he said to them, "Let us go across to the other side of the lake." So they put out, and while they were sailing he fell asleep. A wind-storm swept down on the lake, and the boat was filling with water, and they were in danger. They went to him and woke him up, shouting, "Master, we are perishing!" And he woke up and rebuked the wind and the raging waves; they ceased, and there was a calm. He said to them, "Where is your faith?" They were afraid and amazed, and said to one another, "Who then is this, that he commands even the winds and the water, and they obey him?"' Luke 8:22-26

Islam

'You who believe! Bow down and prostrate yourselves, and worship your Lord, and do good, that happily you may prosper.' 22:77

'Lord of the heavens and the earth and all this is in between them! Therefore, worship Him and be steadfast in His service.' 19:65

'Hymn the praise of your Lord, and be of those who prostrate themselves (before Him).' 15:98

'He who turns away from remembrance of Me, his will be a narrow life, and I shall bring him blind to the assembly on the Day of Resurrection.' 20:124

'The dwellers of the Fire [people in hell] ... took their religion for a sport and a pastime.' 7:50-51

Judaism

'You shall be holy, for I, the lord your God, am holy.' Leviticus 19:2

'God called to him [Moses] out of the bush, "Moses, Moses!" And he said, "Here I am." Then he said, "Come no closer! Remove the sandals from your feet, for the place on which you are standing is holy ground" .... Moses said to God, "If I come to the Israelites and say to them, 'The God of your ancestors has sent me to you,' and they ask me, 'What is his name?' what shall I say to them?" God said to Moses, "I am who I am .... This is my name forever, and this my title for all generations."'
From Exodus 3:4-5, 13-14, 15b

Christianity

'Therefore I [Jesus] tell you, people will be forgiven for every sin and blasphemy, but blasphemy against the Spirit will not be forgiven. Whoever speaks a word against the Son of Man [Jesus] will be forgiven, but whoever speaks against the Holy Spirit will not be forgiven, either in this age or in the age to come.'
Matthew 12:31-32

Islam

'I seek refuge in You, my Lord.' 23:98

'In Allah let believers put their trust.' 5:11

'In Him do I put my trust, and in Him let all the trusting put their trust.' 12:67

'Truly in the remembrance of Allah do hearts find rest.' 13:28

'In You we put our trust, and to You we turn repentant, and unto You is the journeying.' 60:4

'Praise to Allah who put grief away from us. Our Lord is Forgiving, Bountiful.' 35:34

Judaism

'The Lord gave and the Lord has taken away; blessed be the name of the Lord.' Job 1:21

'Blessed are those who trust in the Lord, whose trust is the Lord. They shall be like a tree planted by water, sending out its roots by the stream. It shall not fear when heat comes, and its leaves shall stay green; in the year of drought it is not anxious, and it does not cease to bear fruit.' Jeremiah 17:7-8

'Have you not known? Have you not heard? The Lord is the everlasting God, the Creator of the ends of the earth.' Isaiah 40:28

Christianity

'Ask and it will be given you; search, and you will find; knock, and the door will be opened for you. For everyone who asks, receives, and everyone who searches finds, and for everyone who knocks, the door will be opened. Is there anyone among you who, if your child asks for bread, will give a stone? Or if the child asks for a fish, will give a snake? If you then, who are evil, know how to give good gifts to your children, how much more will your Father in heaven give good things to those who ask him!' Matthew 7:7-11

'What have you that you did not receive?' 1 Corinthians 4:7

Islam

'The (true) believers are those only who believe in Allah and His messenger and afterward do not doubt, but strive with their wealth and their lives for the cause of Allah. Such are the sincere.' 49:15

'If your fathers, and your sons, and your brethren, and your wives, and your tribe, and the wealth you have acquired, and merchandise for which you fear that there will be no sale, and dwellings you desire, are dearer to you than Allah and his messenger in striving in His way: then wait till Allah brings His command to pass. Allah does not guide wrong-doing people.' 9:24

'My worship and my sacrifice and my living and my dying are for Allah, Lord of the Worlds.' 6:162

Judaism

'The Lord said: ... these people draw near with their mouths and honour me with their lips, while their hearts are far from me, and their worship of me is a human commandment learned by rote.' Isaiah 29:13

'I, the Lord your God, am a jealous God.' Exodus 20:5

Christianity

'Then Jesus told his disciples, "If any want to become my followers, let them deny themselves and take up their cross and follow. For those who want to save their life will lose it, and those who lose their life for my sake will find it."' Matthew 16:24-25

'I know your works; you are neither hot nor cold. I wish that you were either cold or hot. So, because you are lukewarm, and neither cold nor hot, I am about to spit you out of my mouth.' Revelation 3:15-16

'Live in love, as Christ loved us and gave himself up for us.' Ephesians 5:2

'Peter and the apostles answered, "We must obey God rather than any human authority." As they left the council, they rejoiced that they were considered worthy to suffer dishonour for the sake of the name [of Jesus].' Acts 5:29, 41

Islam

'Glory be to Him in Whose hand is the dominion over all things!' 36:83

'Blessed be He to Whom belongs the Sovereignty of the heavens and the earth and all that is between them, and with Whom is knowledge of the Hour, and to Whom you will be returned.' 43:85

'Blessed be the name of your Lord, Mighty and Glorious!' 55:78

'If you give thanks, I will give you more.' 14:7

'Hymn the praise of your Lord before the rising and before the setting of the sun; and in the night-time hymn His praise, and after the prostrations.' 50:39-40

'Praise be to Allah, the Creator of the heavens and the earth.' 35:1

'Praise the name of your Lord, the Most High, Who creates, then disposes; Who measures, then guides.' 87:1-3

Judaism

'Praise the Lord, all you nations! Extol him, all you peoples! For great is his steadfast love toward us, and the faithfulness of the Lord endures forever. Praise the Lord!' Psalm 117

Praise the Lord! Praise God in his sanctuary; praise him in his mighty firmament! Praise him for his mighty deeds; praise him according to his surpassing greatness! Praise him with trumpet sound; praise him with lute and harp! Praise him with tambourine and dance; praise him with strings and pipe! Praise him with clanging cymbals; praise him with loud clashing cymbals! Let everything that breathes praise the Lord! Praise the Lord!' Psalm 150

Christianity

'He [Jesus] was praying in a certain place, and after he had finished, one of his disciples said to him, "Lord, teach us to pray, as John taught his disciples." He said to them, "When you pray, say: Father, hallowed be your name. Your kingdom come. Give us each day our daily bread. And forgive us our sins, for we ourselves forgive everyone indebted to us. And do not bring us to the time of trial."' Luke 11:1-4

'Sing psalms and hymns and spiritual songs among yourselves, singing and making melody to the Lord in your hearts, giving thanks to God the Father at all times and for everything in the name of our Lord Jesus Christ.' Ephesians 5:19-20

Islam

'Allah is the Most Merciful of those who show mercy.' 12:92

'Good deeds annul evil deeds.' 11:114

'On the Day of Resurrection ... every soul will be paid in full what it has earned; and they will not be wronged.' 3:161

'Those who point at such of the believers as give the alms willingly ... and deride them, Allah (Himself) derides them. Theirs will be a painful doom.' 9:79

'Allah promises ... the disbelievers fire of hell for their abode ... Allah curses them, and theirs is lasting torment.' 9:68

'Ask forgiveness for them, (Muhammad) or ask not forgiveness for them; though you ask forgiveness for them seventy times, Allah will not forgive them. That is because they disbelieved in Allah and His messenger, and Allah does not guide wrong-doing people.' 9:79-80

'Do not despair of the mercy of Allah, Who forgives all sins.' 39:53

'God does not judge you according to your appearance and your wealth, but He looks at your hearts and looks into your deeds.' Saheeh Muslim, no. 2564

Judaism

'The Lord does not see as mortals see; they look on the outward appearance, but the Lord looks on the heart.'
1 Samuel 16:7

'How can a mortal be righteous before God? How can one born of woman be pure? If even the moon is not bright and the stars are not pure in his sight, how much less a mortal, who is a maggot, and a human being, who is a worm!'
Job 25:4-6

'Many of those who sleep in the dust of the earth shall awake, some to everlasting life, and some to shame and everlasting contempt.' Daniel 12:2

Christianity

'When the Son of Man [Jesus] comes in his glory, and all the angels with him, then he will sit on the throne of his glory. All the nations will be gathered before him, and he will separate people one from another as a shepherd separates the sheep from the goats, and he will put the sheep at his right hand and the goats at his left. Then the king will say to those at his right hand, 'Come, you that are blessed by my Father, inherit the kingdom prepared for you from the foundation of the world; for I was hungry and you gave me food, I was thirsty and you gave me something to drink, I was a stranger and you welcomed me, I was naked and you gave me clothing, I was sick and you took care of me, I was in prison and you visited me.' Then the righteous will answer him, 'Lord, when was it that we saw you hungry and gave you food, or thirsty and gave you something to drink? And when was it that we saw you a stranger and welcomed you, or naked and gave you clothing? And when was it that we saw you sick or in prison and visited you?' And the king will answer them, 'Truly, I tell you, just as you did it to one of the least of these who are members of my family, you did it to me.' Then he will say to those at his left hand, 'You that are accursed, depart from me into the eternal fire prepared for the devil and his angels; for I was hungry and you gave me no food, I was thirsty and you gave me nothing to drink, I was a stranger and you did not welcome me, naked and you did not give me clothing, sick and in prison and you did not visit me.' Then they also will answer, 'Lord, when was it that we saw you hungry or thirsty or a stranger or naked or sick or in prison, and did not take care of you?' Then he will answer them, 'Truly I tell you, just as you did not do it to one of the least of these, you did not do it to me.' And these will go away into eternal punishment, but the righteous into eternal life.'

Matthew 25:31-46

A Qur'ân fragment, probably from Baghdad. Early fourteenth century. Chester Beatty Library, Dublin

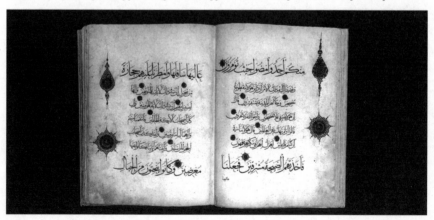

Islam

'Forgive us, our Lord! You, only you, are the Mighty, the Wise.' 60:5

'Allah does not change the condition of a people until they (first) change what is in their hearts. Allah sends whom He will astray, and guides to Himself all who turn (to Him).' 13:11, 27

'Seek forgiveness of Allah. Allah is ever Forgiving, Merciful.' 4:106

'Allah the Almighty has said: O son of Adam, so long as you call upon Me and ask of Me, I shall forgive you for what you have done, and I shall not mind. O son of Adam, were your sins to reach the clouds of the sky and were you then to ask forgiveness of Me, I would forgive you. O son of Adam, were you to come to Me with sins nearly as great as the earth and were you then to face Me, ascribing no partner to Me, I would bring you forgiveness nearly as great as it is.' An-Nawawi, no. 42

Judaism

'If you return to me and keep my commandments and do them, though your outcasts are under the farthest skies, I will gather them from there and bring them to the place I have chosen to establish my name.' Nehemiah 1:9

'Come now, let us argue it out, says the Lord; though your sins are like scarlet, they shall be like snow; though they are red like crimson, they shall become like wool.' Isaiah 1:18

'Who is a God like you, pardoning iniquity and passing over the transgression of the remnant of your possession? He does not retain his anger forever, because he delights in showing clemency. He will again have compassion upon us; he will tread our iniquities under foot. You will cast all our sins into the depths of the sea.' Micah 7:18-19

Christianity

'What woman having ten silver coins, if she loses one of them, does not light a lamp, sweep the house, and search carefully until she finds it? When she has found it, she calls together her friends and neighbours, saying, "Rejoice with me, for I have found the coin that was lost." Just so, I tell you, there is joy in the presence of the angels of God over one sinner who repents.' Luke 15:8-10

'God proved his love for us in that while we were still sinners Christ died for us.' Romans 5:8

A seventeenth-century scroll of the Torah. Chester Beatty Library, Dublin.

Teaching on Human Relations

Islam

'Mankind is one community.' 10:19

Islam

'The believers are nothing else but brothers. Therefore make peace between your brothers and observe your duty to Allah so that happily you may obtain mercy.' 49:10

Judaism

'God created humankind in his image, in the image of God he created them; male and female he created them.' Genesis 1:27

'What race deserves honour? The human race. What race deserves honour? Those who fear the Lord'. Sirach 10:19 (*Jerusalem Bible* version)

'None of you [truly] believes until he wishes for his brother what he wishes for himself.' An-Nawawi, no. 13

Judaism

'This is the covenant that I will make with the house of Israel after those days, says the Lord: I will put my law within them, and I will write it on their hearts; and I will be their God, and they shall be my people.' Jeremiah 31:33

Christianity

'[God] gives to all mortals life and breath. From one ancestor he made all nations to inhabit the whole earth, and he allotted the times of their existence and the boundaries of the places where they should live, so that they would search for God, and perhaps grope for him and find him – though indeed he is not far from each of us. For "In him we live and move and have our being."'
From Acts 17:25-28

'You are a people holy to the Lord your God; the Lord your God has chosen you out of all the peoples on earth to be his people, his treasured possession. It was not because you were more numerous than any other people that the Lord set his heart on you and chose you – for you were the fewest of all peoples. It was because the Lord loved you ...'
Deuteronomy 7:6-8

Christianity

'You are a chosen race, a royal priesthood, a holy nation, God's own people ... Once you were not a people, but now you are God's people.' 1 Peter 2:9, 10

'Indeed, the body does not consist of one member but of many. If the foot would say, "Because I am not a hand I do not belong to the body," that would not make it any less a part of the body .... God arranged the members in the body, each one of them as he chose. As it is, there are many members, but one body .... If one member suffers, all suffer together with it; if one member is honoured, all rejoice with it.'

From 1 Corinthians 12:14-15, 18, 26

The Family

Islam

'Beautified for mankind is love of the joys (that come) from women and offspring.' 3:14

Judaism

'I take pleasure in three things, and they are beautiful in the sight of God and of mortals: agreement among brothers and sisters, friendship among neighbours, and a wife and a husband who live in harmony.' Sirach 25:1

'The Lord honours a father above his children, and he confirms a mother's right over her children. Those who honour their father atone for sins, and those who respect their mother are like those who lay up treasure .... Whoever forsakes a father is like a blasphemer, and whoever angers a mother is cursed by the Lord.' Sirach 3:2-4, 16

Christianity

'People were bringing little children to him in order that he might touch them; and the disciples spoke sternly to them. But when Jesus saw this, he was indignant and said to them, "Let the little children come to me; do not stop them; for it is to such as these that the kingdom of God belongs. Truly I tell you, whoever does not receive the kingdom of God as a little child will never enter it." And he took them up in his arms, laid his hands on them, and blessed them.' Mark 10:13-16

MARRIAGE

Islam

'Men are in charge of women, because Allah made one of them to excel the other .... Good women are the obedient .... As for those from whom you fear rebellion, admonish them and banish them to beds apart, and scourge them.' 4:34

'Marry of the women who seem good to you, two or three or four.' 4:3

'You will not be able to deal equally between wives, however much you may wish.' 4:129

'And if you fear a breach between the two (husband and wife), appoint an arbiter from his people and an arbiter from her people. If they desire amendment, Allah will make them of one mind.' 4:35

'The most perfect of the believers in faith are the best of them in morals. And the best among them are those who are best to their wives.'
Mosnad Ahmad, no. 7354

Judaism

'Let me see your face, let me hear your voice; for your voice is sweet, and your face is lovely. My beloved is mine and I am his. Upon my bed at night I sought him whom my soul loves; I sought him, but found him not; I called him but he gave no answer.

Set me as a seal upon your heart, as a seal upon your arm; for love is as strong as death, passion fierce as the grave. Its flashes are flashes of fire, a raging flame. Many waters cannot quench love, neither can floods drown it. If one offered for love all the wealth of his house, it would be utterly scorned.'
Song of Solomon 2:14, 16; 3:1; 8:6-8

'I will take you for my wife forever; I will take you for my wife in righteousness and in justice, in steadfast love and in mercy. I will take you for my wife in faithfulness; and you shall know the Lord'. Hosea 2:19-20

Christianity

'Be subject to one another out of reverence for Christ. Wives, be subject to your husbands as you are to the Lord. For the husband is the head of the wife just as Christ is the head of the church, the body of which he is the Saviour. Just as the church is subject to Christ, so also wives ought to be, in everything, to their husbands.

Husbands, love your wives, just as Christ loved the church and gave himself up for her .... Husbands should love their wives as they love their own bodies. He who loves his wife loves himself. For no one ever hates his own body, but he nourishes it and tenderly cares for it, just as Christ does for the church, because we are members of his body ... Each of you should love his wife as himself, and a wife should respect her husband.'
From Ephesians 5:21-25, 28-30, 33

Islam

'Your Lord has decreed ... (that you show) kindness to parents. If one of them or both of them attain old age with you, do not speak badly to them or repulse them, but speak to them a gracious word .... My Lord, have mercy on them both as they did care for me when I was little.' 17:23

'(Show) kindness to parents, and to near relatives, and orphans, and the needy, and to the neighbour who is kin (to you) and the neighbour who is not of kin, and the fellow-traveller and the wayfarer and (the slaves) whom your right hands possess.' 4:36

'Be careful of your duty ... towards the wombs (that bore you).' 4:1

'A man came to the Prophet Muhammad and said, "Messenger of God! Who among the people is the most worthy of my good companionship?" The Prophet said, "Your mother." The man said, "Then who?" The Prophet said, "Then your mother." The man further asked, "Then who?" The Prophet said, "Then your mother." The man asked again, "Then who?" The Prophet said: "Then your father."' Saheeh Muslim, no. 2548

Judaism

'With all your heart honour your father, and do not forget the birth pangs of your mother. Remember that it was of your parents that you were born; how can you repay what they have given to you?' Sirach 7:27-28

'Listen to your father who begot you, and do not despise your mother when she is old. Let your father and mother be glad; let her who bore you rejoice.' Proverbs 23:22, 25

Christianity

'Fathers, do not provoke your children to anger, but bring them up in the discipline and instruction of the Lord.' Ephesians 6:4

'God said, "Honour your father and your mother" ... But you say that whoever tells father or mother, "Whatever support you might have had from me is given to God", then that person need not honour the father. So, for the sake of your own tradition, you make void the word of God. You hypocrites!' From Matthew 15:4-7

WOMEN

Islam

'Male ... female ... you proceed from one another.' 3:195

'Women have rights similar to those (of men) over them in kindness, and men are a degree above them.' 2:228

'As for those of your women who are guilty of lewdness, call to witness four of you against them. And if they testify (to the truth of the allegation) then confine them to the houses until death take them, or (until) Allah appoint for them a way (through new legislation).' 4:15

Judaism

'A woman's beauty lights up a man's face and there is nothing he desires more. If kindness and humility mark her speech, her husband is more fortunate than other men. He who acquires a wife gets his best possession, a helper fit for him and a pillar of support. Where there is no wife, a man will become a fugitive and a wanderer.' *From* Sirach 36:27-30.

'It is better to live in a desert land than with a contentious and fretful wife.' Proverbs 21:19

'Charm is deceitful and beauty is vain, but a woman who fears the Lord is to be praised.' Ecclesiastes 31:30

Christianity

'Now there was a woman who had been suffering from haemorrhages for twelve years; and though she had spent all she had on physicians, no one could cure her. She came up behind him and touched the fringe of his clothes, and immediately her haemorrhage stopped. Then Jesus asked, "Who touched me?" When all denied it, Peter said, "Master, the crowds surround you and press in on you." But Jesus said, "Someone touched me; for I noticed that power had gone out from me." When the woman saw that she could not remain hidden, she came trembling; and falling down before him, she declared in the presence of all the people why she had touched him, and how she had been immediately healed. He said to her, "Daughter, your faith has made you well; go in peace."' Luke 8:43-48

'Mary Magdalene went and announced to the disciples, "I have seen the Lord".' John 20:18

Sexuality

Islam

'Allah forbids lewdness and abomination and wickedness.' 16:90

'Tell believing men to lower their gaze and be modest. That is purer for them .... Tell the believing women ... to draw their veils over their bosoms .... Marry such of you as are solitary .... And let those who cannot find a match keep chaste till Allah give them independence by His grace.' *From* 24:30-33

'Do not consummate the marriage until (the term) prescribed is run.' 2:235

'There is no sin for you in what you do by mutual agreement after the duty (has been done).' 4:24

'The adulterer and the adulteress, scourge each one of them a hundred stripes. And let not pity for the two withold you from obedience to Allah, if you believe in Allah and the Last Day. And let a party of believers witness their punishment.' 24:2

'And those who accuse honourable women but do not bring four witnesses, scourge them eighty stripes, and never (afterwards) accept their testimony.' 24:4

Judaism

'The man and his wife [Adam and Eve] were both naked, and were not ashamed.' Genesis 2:25

'You shall not commit adultery.' Exodus 20:14

'You shall not lie with a man as with a woman; it is an abomination.' Leviticus 18:22

Christianity

'Do you not know that your bodies are members of Christ? ... Anyone united to the Lord should become one spirit with him. Shun fornication! Every sin that a person commits is outside the body; but the fornicator sins against the body itself. Or do you not know that your body is a temple of the Holy Spirit within you, which you have from God, and that you are not your own. For you were bought with a price; therefore glorify Christ in your body.' 1 Corinthians 6:15, 17-20

DIVORCE

Islam

'Divorce must be pronounced twice.'
2:229

Judaism

'... a man enters into marriage with a woman, but she does not please him because he finds something objection-able about her, and so he writes her a certificate of divorce, puts it in her hand, and sends her out of the house.'
Deuteronomy 24:1

Christianity

'Anyone who divorces his wife and marries another commits adultery, and whoever marries a woman divorced from her husband commits adultery.' Luke 16:18

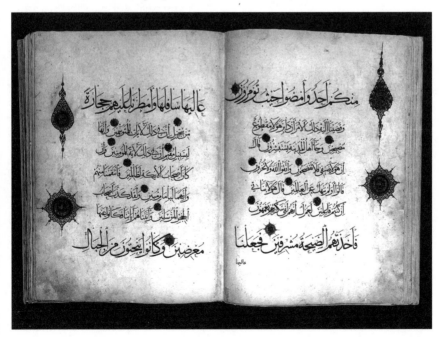

Islam

'A man walking along a path felt very thirsty. Reaching a well, he descended into it, drank his fill, and came up. Then he saw a dog with its tongue hanging out, trying to lick up mud to quench its thirst. The man said, "This dog is feeling the same thirst that I felt." So he went down into the well again, filled his shoe with water, and gave the dog a drink. So, God thanked him and forgave his sins. The Prophet was asked, "Messenger of God, are we rewarded for kindness towards animals?" He said, "There is a reward for kindness to every living animal or human."'
Saheeh Muslim, no. 2244

Judaism

'You shall love your neighbour as yourself; I am the Lord.' Leviticus 19:18

'The merciful lend to their neighbours; by holding out a helping hand they keep the commandments. Lend to your neighbour in his time of need; repay your neighbour when a loan falls due. Keep your promise and be honest with him.' Sirach 29:1-2

Christianity

'I give you a new commandment, that you love one another. Just as I have loved you, you also should love one another. By this everyone will know that you are my disciples, if you have love for one another.' John 13:34-35

'Love is the fulfilling of the law.' Romans 13:10

Islam

'Whoever is patient and forgives, that truly is the steadfast heart of things.' 42:43

'Repel the evil deed with one which is better, then he, between whom and you there was enmity, (will become) as though he was a bosom friend.' 41:34

'The merciful are shown mercy by the All-Merciful. Show mercy to those on earth, and God will show mercy to you.' Al-Tirmizi, no. 1924

Judaism

'Joseph's brothers said, "What if Joseph still bears a grudge against us and pays us back in full for all the wrongs that we did to him?" So they approached Joseph saying, "Please forgive the crime of the servants of the God of your father."

Joseph said to them, "Do not be afraid. Am I in the place of God? Even though you intended to do harm to me, God intended it for good .... so have no fear." In this way he reassured them, speaking kindly to them.' *From* Genesis 50:15-21

Christianity

'Peter came and said to him [Jesus], "Lord, if my brother sins against me, how often should I forgive? As many as seven times?" Jesus said to him, "Not seven times, but, I tell you, seventy-seven times."' Matthew 18:21-22

'If you forgive others their trespasses, your heavenly Father will also forgive you; but if you do not forgive others, neither will your Father forgive your trespasses.' Matthew 6:14-15

Islam

'Fill the measure when you measure, and weigh with a right balance; that is just, and better in the end.' 17:35

'Give your relative his due, and the needy, and the wayfarer, and do not squander (your wealth) in wantonness.' 17:26

'Do not let hatred of any people seduce you so that you do not deal justly. Deal justly, that is nearer to your duty. Observe your duty to Allah. Allah is informed of what you do.' 5:8

'Make peace between them (fighting parties) justly, and act equitably. Allah loves the equitable.' 49:9

'We prescribed for them therein: The life for the life, and the eye for the eye, and the nose for the nose, and the ear for the ear, and the tooth for the tooth, and for wounds retaliation. But whosoever forgoes it, it shall be expiation for him.' 5:45

'As for those who are unjust, they are firewood for hell.' 72:15

'Pay the worker his wage before his sweat dries.' Ibn Majah, no. 2443

Judaism

'Anyone who maims another shall suffer the same injury in return: fracture for fracture, eye for eye, tooth for tooth, the injury inflicted is the injury to be suffered.' Leviticus 24:20

'I the Lord love justice.' Isaiah 61:8

'To do righteousness and justice is more acceptable to the Lord than sacrifice.' Proverbs 21:3

'Can I forget the treasures of wickedness in the house of the wicked, and the scant measure that is accursed? Can I tolerate wicked scales and a bag of dishonest weights? Your wealthy are full of violence; your inhabitants speak lies, with tongues of deceit in their mouths.' Micah 6:10-11

'You must not move your neighbour's boundary marker, set up by former generations.' Deuteronomy 19:14

Christianity

'You have heard that it was said, "An eye for an eye and a tooth for a tooth." But I say to you: Do not resist an evildoer. But if anyone strikes you on the right cheek, turn the other also; and if anyone wants to sue you and take your coat, give your cloak as well; and if anyone forces you to go one mile, go also the second mile. Give to everyone who begs from you, and do not refuse anyone who wants to borrow from you.' Matthew 5:38-42

'Blessed are the peacemakers, for they will be called children of God.' Matthew 5:9

'When you are offering your gift at the altar, if you remember that your brother or sister has something against you, leave your gift before the altar and go; first be reconciled to your brother or sister, and then come and offer your gift.' Matthew 5:23-24

Islam

'Allah forbids usury.' 2:275

'If the debtor is in straitened circumstances, then (let there be) postponement to (the time of) ease; and that you remit the debt as almsgiving would be better for you if you did but know.' 2:280

'If you lend to Allah a goodly loan, He will double it for you and will forgive you, for Allah is Responsive, Clement.' 64:17 (Note: A 'goodly loan' is one without interest or any thought of gain or loss.)

Judaism

'If you lend money to my people, to the poor among you, you shall not deal with them as with a creditor; you shall not exact interest from them. If you take your neighbour's cloak in pawn, you shall restore it before the sun goes down; for it may be your neighbour's only clothing to use as cover; in what else shall that person sleep? And if your neighbour cries out to me, I will listen, for I am compassionate.'
Exodus 22:25-27

'The land shall not be sold in perpetuity, for the land is mine; with me you are but aliens and tenants.' Leviticus 25:23

'If a man is righteous and does what is lawful and right – if he ... does not oppress anyone, but restores to the debtor his pledge, commits no robbery, gives his bread to the hungry and covers the naked with a garment, does not take advance or accrued interest, withholds his hand from iniquity, executes true justice between contending parties, follows my statutes, and is careful to observe my ordinances, acting faithfully – such a one is righteous; he shall surely live, says the Lord God.' *From* Ezekiel 18:5-9

Christianity

'Jesus spoke up and said to him, "Simon, I have something to say to you." "Teacher," he replied, "speak." "A certain creditor had two debtors: one owed five hundred denarii, and the other fifty. When they could not pay, he cancelled the debts for both of them. Now which of them will love him more?" Simon answered, "I suppose the one for whom he cancelled the greater debt." And Jesus said to him, "You have judged rightly ... The one to whom little is forgiven loves little".' *From* Luke 7:40-43, 47

GREED

Islam

'In the love of wealth he (man) is violent.' 100:8

'You do not honour the orphan, and do not urge the feeding of the poor, and you devour heritages with devouring greed, and love wealth with abounding love.' 89:17-20

'On the day when it [gold and silver] will (all) be heated in the fire of Hell, and their foreheads and their flanks and their backs will be branded with it (it will be said to them): "Here is that which you hoarded for yourselves. Now taste what you used to hoard".' 9:35

'Whoever is saved from his own greed, such are the successful.' 64:16

'Let him who has abundance spend of his abundance.' 65:7

Judaism

'Hear this, you that trample on the needy, and bring ruin to the poor of the land, saying, "We will practice deceit with false balances, buying the needy for silver, and the poor for a pair of sandals, and selling the sweepings of the wheat." The Lord has sworn ... "I will never forget any of their deeds."' *From* Amos 8:4-7

'Alas for those who lie on beds of ivory, and lounge on their couches, and eat lambs from the flock, and calves from the stall; who sing idle songs to the sound of the harp ... who drink wine from bowls, and anoint themselves with the finest oils .... They shall now be the first to go into exile, and the revelry of the loungers shall pass away.' *From* Amos 6:4-7

Christianity

'No one can serve two masters; for a slave will either hate the one and love the other, or be devoted to the one and despise the other. You cannot serve God and wealth.' Matthew 6:24

'Jesus said to his disciples, "Truly I tell you, it will be hard for a rich person to enter the kingdom of heaven. Again, I tell you, it is easier for a camel to go through the eye of a needle than for someone who is rich to enter the kingdom of God." When the disciples heard this, they were greatly astounded, and said, "Then who can be saved?" But Jesus looked at them and said, "For mortals it is impossible, but for God all things are possible."' Matthew 19:23-26

'So therefore, none of you can become my disciple if you do not give up all your possessions.' Luke 14:33

GOOD WORKS

Islam

'The orphan oppress not, the beggar drive not away, of the bounty of your Lord be your discourse.' 93:9-11

'Wealth and children are an ornament of life of the world. But the good deeds which endure are better in your Lord's sight for reward, and better in respect of hope.' 18:46

'Those who give alms, both men and women, and lend to Allah a goodly loan, it will be doubled unto them and theirs will be a rich reward.' 57:18

'Compete with one another in good works.' 5:48

'Each person's every joint must perform a charity every day the sun comes up; to act justly between two people is a charity; to help a man with his mount, lifting him onto it or hoisting up his belongings onto it is a charity; every step you take to prayers is a charity; and removing a harmful thing from the road is a charity.' An-Nawawi, no. 26

Judaism

'Since there will never cease to be some in need on the earth, I therefore command you, "Open your hand to the poor and needy neighbour in your land".' Deuteronomy 15:11

'If any of your kin fall into difficulty and become dependent on you, you shall support them.' Leviticus 25:35

'You shall not wrong or oppress a resident alien, for you were aliens in the land of Egypt. You shall not abuse any widow or orphan. If you do abuse them, when they cry out to me, I will surely heed their cry.' Exodus 22:21-23

Christianity

'What good is it, my brothers and sisters, if you say you have faith but do not have works? Can faith save you? If a brother or sister is naked and lacks daily food, and one of you says to them, "Go in peace; keep warm and eat your fill," and yet you do not supply their bodily needs, what is the good of that? So faith by itself, if it has no works, is dead. A person is justified by works and not by faith alone. For just as the body without the spirit is dead, so faith without works is also dead.' James 2:14-17, 24, 26

'When you give alms, do not let your left hand know what your right hand is doing, so that your alms may be done in secret; and your Father who sees in secret will reward you.' Matthew 6:4

Islam

'Whoever goes right, it is for his soul and whoever strays, strays only to its hurt. And (Muhammad) ... you are not a warder over them.' 39:41

'Everyone starts his day and is a vendor of his soul, either freeing it or bringing about its ruin.' An-Nawawi, no. 23

Judaism

'Do not say, "It was the Lord's doing that I fell away"; for he does not do what he hates. Do not say, "It was he who led me astray"; for he has no need of the sinful. The Lord hates all abominations; such things are not loved by those who fear him. It was he who created humankind in the beginning, and he left them in the power of their own free choice. If you choose, you can keep the commandments, and to act faithfully is a matter of your own choice. He has placed before you fire and water; stretch out your hand for whichever you choose. Before each person are life and death, and whichever he chooses will be given. For great is the wisdom of the Lord; he is mighty in power and sees everything; his eyes are on those who fear him, and he knows every human action. He has not commanded anyone to be wicked, and he has not given anyone permission to sin.' Sirach 15:11-20

Christianity

'Each of us will be accountable to God.' Romans 14:12

'All must carry their own loads.' Galatians 6:5

Islam

'No laden one shall bear another's load. Man has only that for which he makes effort.' 53:38-39

Judaism

'The Lord took the man and put him in the garden to till it and keep it.' Genesis 2:15

'People go out to their work and to their labour until the evening. O Lord, how manifold are your works! In wisdom you have made them all.' Psalm 104:23-24

Christianity

'Whatever you do, in word or in deed, do everything in the name of the Lord Jesus, giving thanks to God the Father through him.' Colossians 3:17

'Anyone unwilling to work should not eat.' 2 Thessalonians 3:10

Islam

'Fight in the way of Allah against those who fight against you, but do not begin hostilities. Allah does not love aggressors.' 2:190

Judaism

'He [the Lord] shall judge between many peoples, and shall arbitrate between strong nations far away; they shall beat their swords into ploughshares, and their spears into pruning hooks; nation shall not lift up sword against nation, neither shall they learn war any more; but they shall all sit under their own vines and under their own fig trees, and no one shall make them afraid; for the mouth of the Lord of hosts has spoken.' Micah 4:3-4

Christianity

'You have heard that it was said, "You shall love your neighbour and hate your enemy." But I say to you, Love your enemies and pray for those who persecute you, so that you may be children of your Father in heaven.' Matthew 5:43-45

STEALING

Islam

'Whoever is forced by hunger, not by will, to sin: (for him) Allah is Forgiving, Merciful.' 5:3

'As for the thief, both male and female, cut off their hands.' 5:38

Judaism

'You shall not steal.' Exodus 20:15

'I the Lord ... hate robbery and wrong-doing.' Isaiah 61:8

Christianity

'The commandments, "You shall not commit adultery; You shall not murder; You shall not steal; You shall not covet"; and any other commandment, are summed up in this word, "Love your neighbour as yourself." Love does no wrong to a neighbour; therefore love is the fulfilling of the law.' Romans 13:9

'Thieves must give up stealing; rather let them labour and work honestly with their own hands, so as to have some-thing to share with the needy.' Ephesians 4:28

SLAVERY

Islam

'Such of your slaves as ask a writing (of emancipation), write it for them if you are aware of good in them, and bestow on them of the wealth of Allah which He has bestowed on you. Do not force your slave-girls to whoredom .... And if one forces them, then (to them), after their compulsion, Allah will be Forgiving, Merciful. 24:33

Judaism

'When you buy a male Hebrew slave, he shall serve six years, but in the seventh he shall go out a free person, without debt.' Deuteronomy 21:2

'The word ... came to Jeremiah from the Lord ... that all should set free their Hebrew slaves, male and female, so that no one should hold another Judean in slavery.' *From* Jeremiah 34:8-9

Christianity

'Let each of you lead the life that the Lord has assigned, to which God called you ... Were you a slave when called? Do not be concerned about it .... In whatever condition you were called, brothers and sisters, there remain with God.' 1 Corinthians 7:17, 21, 24

Christianity

Jesus said to them, 'It is not what goes into the mouth that defiles a person, but it is what comes out the mouth that defiles .... Are you still without under-standing? Do you not see that whatever goes into the mouth enters the stomach and goes out into the sewer? But what comes out of the mouth proceeds from the heart, and this is what defiles. For out of the heart come evil intentions, murder, adultery, fornication, theft, false witness, slander. These are what defile a person ...' Matthew 15:11, 16-20

'Do not get drunk with wine, for that is debauchery; but be filled with the Spirit.' Ephesians 5:18

Islam

'Strong drink and games of chance and idols and divining arrows are only an infamy of Satan's handiwork. Leave it aside in order that you may succeed.' 5:90

Judaism

'Go, eat your bread with enjoyment, and drink your wine with a merry heart; for God has long ago approved what you do.' Ecclesiastes 9:7

'Be drunk, but not from wine.' Isaiah 29:9

Teaching on relations with those of other faiths and of none

Islam

'Unto you your religion, and unto me my religion.' 109:6

'Whosoever seeks as religion other than the Surrender (to Allah), it will not be accepted from him, and he will be a loser in the Hereafter.' 3:85 (Note: 'The Surrender', in Arabic, is Al-Islam.)

'Obey Allah and obey His messenger; but if you turn away, then the duty of Our messenger is only to convey (the message) plainly.' 64:12

'When you go forth in the land, it is no sin for you to curtail worship if you fear that those who disbelieve may attack you.' 4:101

Judaism

'When a foreigner, who is not of your people Israel, comes from a distant land because of your name ... when a foreigner comes and prays towards this house, then hear in heaven your dwelling place, and do according to all that the foreigner calls to you, so that all the peoples of the earth may know your name and fear you.' 1 Kings 8:41-43

Christianity

'Because of this [teaching] many of his [Jesus'] disciples turned back and no longer went about with him. So Jesus asked the twelve, "Do you also wish to go away?" John 6:66-67

God is 'the Lord of the harvest.' Matthew 9:37

JESUS

Islam

'They (the Christians) say: "The Beneficent has taken to Himself a son." Assuredly you utter a disastrous thing, whereby almost the heavens are torn, and the earth is split asunder and the mountains fall in ruins, that you ascribe unto the Beneficent a son, when it is not right for (the Majesty of) the Beneficent that He should choose a son.' 19:88-92

'O People of the Scripture! Do not exaggerate in your religion nor utter anything concerning Allah save the truth. The Messiah, Jesus son of Mary, was only a messenger of Allah, and his word which he conveyed unto Mary, and a spirit from Him. So believe in Allah and His messengers, and do not say 'Three' – Cease! (it is) better for you! Allah is only one God. Far is it removed from his transcendent majesty that He should have a son. His is all that is in the heavens and all that is in the earth. And Allah is sufficient as Defender.' 4:171

'The Messiah, son of Mary, was no other than a messenger, messengers (the like of whom) had passed away before him. And his mother was a saintly woman.' 5:75

'Jesus son of Mary said: "Children of Israel! I am the messenger of Allah unto you, confirming what was (revealed) before me in the Torah and bringing good tidings of a messenger who comes after me, whose name is the Praised One".' 61:6

Judaism

The Jewish scriptures, or Old Testament, were written centuries before the time of Jesus.

Christianity

'They shall name him "Emmanuel," which means "God is with us".' Matthew 1:23

'The Word became flesh and lived among us.' John 1:14

'[Christ] is the image of the invisible God, the first born of all creation; for in him all things in heaven and on earth were created, things visible and invisible ... all things have been created through him and for him. He himself is before all things, and in him all things hold together. He is the head of the body, the church; he is the beginning, the firstborn from the dead, so that he might come to have first place in everything. For in him all the fullness of God was pleased to dwell, and through him God was pleased to reconcile to himself all things, whether on earth or in heaven, by making peace through the blood of his cross.' Colossians 1:15-20

Islam

'Say [to Jews and Christians]: We believe in that which has been revealed to us and revealed to you; our God and your God is One, and to Him we surrender.' 29:46

'We caused Jesus, son of Mary, to follow, and gave him the Gospel, and placed compassion and mercy in the hearts of those who followed him. But monasticism they invented – We did not ordain it for them – only seeking Allah's pleasure, and they observed it not with right observance .... Many of them are evil-livers.' 57:27

'Take not the Jews and Christians for friends. They are friends to one another. He among you who takes them for friends is of them.' 5:51

'Repel not those who call upon their Lord at morn and evening, seeking His Face. You are not accountable for them in anything, nor are they accountable to you for anything.' 6:52

'He it is who has sent His messenger with the guidance and the Religion of Truth, that He may cause it to prevail over all religions.' 9:33

'Those who believe, and those who are Jews, and ... Christians – whoever believes in Allah and the Last Day and does right –

there shall no fear come upon them, neither shall they grieve.' 5:69

Judaism

'The compassion of human beings is for their neighbours, but the compassion of the Lord is for every living thing. He rebukes and trains and teaches them, and turns them back, as a shepherd his flock. He has compassion on those who accept his discipline and who are eager for his precepts.' Sirach 18:13-14

Christianity

'There is no longer Jew and Greek, circumcised and uncircumcised, barbarian, Scythian, slave and free; but Christ is all in all!' Colossians 3:11

'Maintain the unity of the Spirit in the bond of peace. There is one body and one Spirit, just as you were called to the one hope of your calling, one Lord, one faith, one baptism, one God and Father of all, who is above all and through all and in all.' Ephesians 4:3-6

'To those who are sanctified in Christ Jesus, called to be saints, together with all those who in every place call on the name of our Lord Jesus Christ, both their Lord and ours: Grace to you and peace from God our Father and the Lord Jesus Christ.' 1 Corinthians 1:2-3

Relations with disbelievers

Islam

'Would you (Muhammad) compel men until they are believers? It is not for any soul to believe save by permission of Allah.' 10:99-100

'Give a respite to the disbelievers. Deal gently with them for a while.' 86:17

'Muhammad is the messenger of Allah, and those with him are hard against the disbelievers and merciful among themselves.' 48:29

'As for those who disbelieve, garments of fire will be cut out for them; boiling fluid will be poured down on their heads. Their skins, too, will be melted. For them are hooked rods of iron. Whenever, in their anguish, they would go forth from there they are driven back in and (it is said to them): "Taste the doom of burning".' 22:19-22

'Most of mankind refuse anything except disbelief.' 17:89

Judaism

'In days to come ... they shall all sit under their own vines and under their own fig trees, and no one shall make them afraid; for the mouth of the Lord has spoken.' Micah 4:1, 4

'Thus says the Lord God, who gathers the outcasts of Israel, I will gather others to them besides those already gathered.' Isaiah 56:8

Christianity

Jesus said to his disciples: 'Go into all the world and proclaim the good news to the whole creation. The one who believes and is baptised will be saved; but the one who does not believe will be condemned.' Mark 16:15-16

John said, 'Master, we saw someone casting out demons in your name, and we tried to stop him, because he does not follow with us.' But Jesus said to him, 'Do not stop him; for whoever is not against you is for you.' Luke 9:49-50

'Peter began to speak to them: "I truly understand that God shows no partiality, but in every nation anyone who fears him and does what is right is acceptable to him."' Acts 10:34-35

'All who have not believed the truth but took pleasure in unrighteousness will be condemned.' 2 Thessalonians 2:12

'Anyone, then, who knows the right thing to do and fails to do it, commits sin.' James 4:17

Teaching on the things to come

PERSEVERANCE

Islam

'Those who persevere and do good works ... theirs will be forgiveness and a great reward.' 11:11

'You who believe! Endure, outdo all others in endurance.' 3:200

'You who believe! Seek help in steadfastness and prayer. Allah is with the steadfast.' 2:153

Judaism

'O that my ways may be steadfast in keeping your statutes!' Psalm 119:5

'Happy are those who persevere.' Daniel 12:12

Christianity

'The one who endures to the end will be saved.' Matthew 24:13

'A thorn was given me in the flesh, a messenger of Satan to torment me, to keep me from being too elated. Three times I appealed to the Lord about this, that it would leave me, but he said to me, "My grace is sufficient for you, for power is made perfect in weakness." So, I will boast all the more gladly of my weaknesses, so that the power of Christ may dwell in me. Therefore I am content with weaknesses, insults, hardships, persecutions, and calamities for the sake of Christ; for when I am weak, then I am strong.' 2 Corinthians 12:7-10

Islam

'Do not say of anything: "I shall do that tomorrow", except if Allah will.' 18:23-24

'At evening do not expect morning, and at morning do not expect evening.' An-Nawawi, no. 40

'Whatever God wills to happen happens, and whatever He wills not to happen does not happen.' Ibrahim, page 49

Judaism

'For everything there is a season, and a time for every matter under heaven:
a time to be born, and a time to die;
a time to plant, and a time to pluck up what is planted;
a time to kill, and a time to heal;
a time to break down, and a time to build up;
a time to weep, and a time to laugh;
a time to mourn, and a time to dance;
a time to throw away stones, and a time to gather stones together;
a time to embrace, and a time to refrain from embracing;
a time to seek, and a time to lose;
a time to keep, and a time to throw away;
a time to tear, and a time to sew;
a time to keep silence, and a time to speak;
a time to love, and a time to hate;
a time for war, and a time for peace.'
Ecclesiastes 3:1-8

'In days to come the mountain of the Lord's house shall be established as the highest of the mountains, and shall be raised above the hills. Peoples shall stream to it, and many nations shall come and say: "Come, let us go up to the mountain of the Lord, to the house of the God of Jacob; that he may teach us his ways and that we may walk in his paths".' Micah 4:1-2

Christianity

'Do not worry about tomorrow, for tomorrow will bring worries of its own. Today's trouble is enough for today.' Matthew 6:34

'Come now, you who say, "Today or tomorrow we will go to such and such a town and spend a year there doing business and making money." Yet you do not even know what tomorrow will bring ... Instead you ought to say, "If the Lord wishes, we will live and do this or that".' James 4:13, 15

Islam

'No soul can ever die except by Allah's leave and at a term appointed.' 3:145

Judaism

'Who can live and never see death? Lord, where is your steadfast love of old? ... Blessed be the Lord forever. Amen and Amen.' Psalm 89:48, 52

'I have no pleasure in the death of anyone, says the Lord God. Turn, then, and live.' Ezekiel 18:32

'The Lord of hosts ... will swallow up death for ever.' Isaiah 25:6-7

Christianity

Jesus said: 'Very truly, I tell you, anyone who hears my word and believes him who sent me has eternal life, and does not come under judgment, but has passed from death to life.' John 5:24

'Where, O death, is your victory? Where, O death, is your sting? Thanks be to God, who gives us the victory through our Lord Jesus Christ'.
1 Corinthians 15:55, 57

Islam

'It is not for the Prophet, and those who believe, to pray for the forgiveness of idolaters even though they may be near relatives after it has become clear that they are people of Hell-fire.' 9:113

'But for those who disbelieve Our revelations, their place will be on the left hand. Fire will be an awning over them.' 90:19-20

'Lo! hell lurks in ambush, a home for the rebellious. They will abide therein for ages. Therein they taste neither coolness nor (any) drink, save boiling water and a paralysing cold: reward proportioned (to their evil deeds). For lo! they looked not for a reckoning. They called our revelations false with strong denial. Everything have We recorded in a Book. So taste (of that which you have earned). No increase do We give you save of torment.' 78:21-30

Judaism

'They shall go out and look at the dead bodies of the people who have rebelled against me; for their worm shall not die, their fire shall not be quenched, and they shall be an abhorrence to all flesh.' Isaiah 66:24

Christianity

'These [who do not obey the gospel] will suffer the punishment of eternal destruction, separated from the presence of the Lord and from the glory of his might.' 2 Thessalonians 1:9

'It is better for you to enter the kingdom of God with one eye than to have two eyes and to be thrown into hell, where their worm never dies, and the fire is never quenched.' Mark 9:47-48

HEAVEN

Islam

'He will forgive you your sins and bring you into ... Gardens of Eden.' 61:12

'In Paradise there are things which no eye has seen, no ear has heard, and the human mind has not thought of.' Saheeh Muslim, no. 2825

Judaism

'For if he [Judas Maccabaeus] were not expecting that those who had fallen would rise again, it would have been superfluous and foolish to pray for the dead. But if he was looking to the splendid reward that is laid up for those who fall asleep in godliness, it was a holy and pious thought. Therefore he made atonement for the dead, so that they might be delivered from their sin.' 2 Maccabees 12:44-45

'Many of those who sleep in the dust of the earth shall awake, some to everlasting life, and some to shame and everlasting contempt. Those who are wise shall shine like the brightness of the sky, and those who lead many to righteousness, like the stars forever and ever.' Daniel 12:2-3

Job said, 'I know that my Redeemer lives, and that at the last he will stand upon the earth; and after my skin has been thus destroyed, then in my flesh I shall see God, whom I shall see on my side, and my eyes shall behold, and not another.' Job 19:25-27

Christianity

'We do not want you to be uninformed, brothers and sisters, about those who have died, so that you may not grieve as others do who have no hope. For since we believe that Jesus died and rose again, even so, through Jesus, God will bring with him all those who have died.' 1 Thessalonians 4:13-14

'See, the home of God is among mortals. He will dwell with them as their God; they will be his peoples, and God himself will be with them; he will wipe away every tear from their eyes. Death will be no more; mourning and crying and pain will be no more ...' Revelation 21:3-4

Acknowledgements

The Bible quotations contained herein are from the *New Revised Standard Version Bible: Catholic Edition,* copyright 1989 by the Division of Christian Education of the National Council of the Churches of Christ in the USA. Used by permission. All rights reserved. There was one exception, namely, the quotation of Sirach 10.19, taken from *The Jerusalem Bible*, published and copyright 1966, 1967 and 1968 by Darton, Longman and Todd Ltd and Doubleday & Co Inc, and used by permission of the publishers.

Citations of Qur'ânic translations are from *The Meaning of the Glorious Qur'ân: an explanatory translation,* by Mohammad Marmaduke Pickthall, Al-Birr Foundation, P.O. Box 12859, London E10 6UN. Some citations from *hadith* are from *A Brief Illustrated Guide to Understanding Islam*, 2nd ed., I. A. Ibrahim, Darussalam, Houston, Texas, USA, 1997. For the sake of brevity it is cited in the text as Ibrahim. Others are from An-Nawawi, *Forty Hadith: an anthology of the sayings of the prophet Muhammad*, trans. by Ezzedin Ibrahim and Denys Johnson-Davies, The Holy Koran Publishing House, P.O. Box 7492, Beirut, Lebanon, 1976. This text is cited as An-Nawawi; the number given is the number of the *hadith* as listed therein.

I wish to express my thanks to the following for their generous help:
Dr Abdul-Ali Hamid, The Muslim College, London;
Imam Al-Hussein, The Islamic Foundation of Ireland, Dublin;
The Chief Rabbinate of Ireland, Dublin;
The Rev Jonathan Gorsky, Jews' College, London;
The Rev Matthew Clerkin, Capuchin Friars, Wellington, New Zealand.

Glossary of terms

Allah, Al-Lah: God, or The God, in Arabic.

Al-Tirmizi: see Hadith.

An-Nawawi: see Hadith.

Gospel: One of the accounts by Matthew, Mark, Luke or John of the life, death and resurrection of Jesus Christ. They form the first and largest part of the (Christian) New Testament. The word comes from the Anglo-Saxon God's spel, meaning God's story.

Hadith: Reliably transmitted report(s) by the prophet Muhammad's companions of what he said, did, or approved of, and understood as explaining the divine message. The hadith is found in various collections such as Al-Tirmizi, An-Nawawi, Ibn Majah, Mosnad Ahmad, Saheeh Al-Bukhari and Saheeh Muslim.

Ibn Majah: see Hadith.

Islam: Al-Islâm, in Arabic, means surrender, referring to the believers' surrender to God.

Koran: see Qur'ân.

Mosnad Ahmad: see Hadith.

Muhammad: Born in Mecca on the Arabian peninsula, he lived from 570 to 632 of the Common Era. About 616 he claimed to be a prophet to whom God was revealing the Qur'ân. Persecuted in Mecca, he fled to Medina in 622. His flight, the Hegira, marks the beginning of the Islamic era. By the time of his death Islam had spread throughout Arabia.

Muslim: In Arabic, one who surrenders (to God). A follower of the Islamic religion.

Qur'ân: In Arabic, literally, a reading; the book believed by Muslims to have been dictated by God to the prophet Muhammad when he was in a trance in various places, principally at Mekkah (Mecca), and at Al-Madînah, (Medina).

Ramadan: the ninth month of the Muslim year, during which strict fasting is enjoined on Muslims.

Saheeh Al-Bukhari: see Hadith.

Saheeh Muslim: see Hadith.

Spirit, The holy: in the Qur'ân, this refers to the angel Gabriel.

Sunnah: What the prophet Muhammad said, did, or approved of.

Surâh: A chapter of the Qur'ân.

Torah: In Hebrew, the word means a teaching, precept or guidance. In the Old Testament, it refers either to the Pentateuch, that is, the first five books of the Bible, or the entire Old Testament.

Zakat: A tax at a fixed rate in proportion to the worth of property collected from the well-to-do and distributed among poor Muslims.